STRANGE
SASKATCHEWAN

CARSON DEMMANS
ILLUSTRATED BY JASON SYLVESTRE

INTRODUCTION

If Frank Anderson (the legendary Saskatchewan publisher, writer and editor) and Robert Ripley of *Ripley's Believe It or Not* had a child, it would look like this book.

It is a tribute to the artistic ability of Jason Sylvestre that he knew exactly what I meant when I told him that this was the vision for this book.

The rest of you will probably need an explanation.

I never met Robert Ripley but I am a huge fan of the comic panel that still bears his name. He was a pioneer in the area of entertaining with strange, interesting and bizarre "true fact" cartoons.

I was, however, lucky enough to know Frank Anderson, a true maverick if there ever was one. A writer, editor, publisher and printer, he was also my neighbour. When I was growing up, he kindly gave me dozens of his non-fiction books full of strange but true stories from all over Western Canada. I've been corrupted ever since.

The book is therefore a tribute to two great influences, Saskatchewan's own Frank Anderson and Ripley, a giant from a hundred years ago.

Enjoy.

Carson Demmans

STRANGE SASKATCHEWAN

THE SHIP THAT NEVER SAILS!

In the 1940s, farmer Tom Sukanen decided he was going to return home to Finland. Despite the fact that Saskatchewan is a landlocked province with no access to the sea, he tore down his barn and built a ship 41 feet long, 28 feet high, and 13 feet long!

Although he worked alone and used handmade tools with improvised materials, experts said the ship was seaworthy, and it is now part of the Sukanen Ship Pioneer Village Museum near Moose Jaw, which also includes antique buildings, artifacts, and machinery.

SERIAL SASKATCHEWAN

JOHN CRAWFORD

DAVID THREINEN

Saskatchewan's only two serial killers shared many similarities. David William Threinen confessed to four murders in Saskatoon and had previously been convicted of murdering a 16 year old girl in Lethbridge Alberta.

John Martin Crawford was convicted of three murders in Saskatoon of which one victim was 16 years old, and was suspected of killing at least one other victim in Saskatoon, bringing his total to four in that city. He was previously convicted of killing a girl in Lethbridge Alberta.

ALIENS ON THE PRAIRIES!

On September, 19, 1963, four Saskatoon children saw a floating figure up to nine feet tall floating above the ground with white skin and robes like a monk! Although many UFO investigators believe it to be a close encounter of the third kind with an alien, the people involved refuse to discuss the incident.

CENTURIES OLD MONSTER!

The legend of the Turtle Lake Monster goes back to Cree legends of a mysterious beast that made people disappear in the Turtle Lake area. It is still seen occasionally up to the present day, although descriptions vary and witnesses say the beast may have the head of a dog, pig or horse!

DOBBERVILLE

DOBBERVILLE?! MAYBE IT'S ONE OF THOSE NEW SUBURBS!

Legendary Saskatchewan Roughrider Glenn Dobbs was so popular in the 1950's that Dobberville became the unofficial name of Regina and mail addressed to Dobber-Ville was still delivered to Regina by Canada Post.

Actor Leslie Nielsen was born in Regina, Saskatchewan, but one of his most famous roles was not seen in his native country for more than 20 years! When he played an American Revolutionary War hero called the Swamp Fox in eight episodes of Wonderful World of Disney, the shows were banned from broadcast because it depicted the Loyalists, who were loyal to Britain and eventually moved to Canada, as being villains!

GIANT AMONG MEN!

HOLD ON A SECOND. I TOLD YOU THAT WAS HOW WE WERE SUPPOSED TO DO IT!

It has been estimated that 110 billion people have lived in the history of the world, but there are only 14 men who have been verified as standing more than eight feet tall, and one of them was Edouard Beaupre of Willowbunch, Saskatchewan. The oldest of 20 children, he had wanted to be a cowboy but was too tall to ride a horse and instead became a circus performer who could lift a 900 pound horse! He lived from 1883 to 1904, but was not buried until 1989 as his body was put on display by circuses and universities until it was finally given to his family for cremation!

GO NORTH TO GET WARM!

On February 1, 2011, it was minus 35 degrees Celsius in Regina, Saskatchewan. The average temperature in Stockhom, Sweden on February 1 from 2006 to 2011 was between minus 3^0 and minus 1^0 Celsius. Stockholm is approximately 600 miles closer to the north pole than Regina!

GET LOST?!

Have you ever tried to find Mourey or Pile o' Bones on a map of Saskatchewan? You can't because they no longer exist!

Mourey changed it's name to Titanic in honor of the famous ship, and Pile o' Bones changed its name to the more dignified Regina. Ironically, Titanic no longer exists either, and the Hamlet is deserted!

On June 13, 1970, lightning struck a telephone pole in rural Saskatchewan. The lightning travelled half a mile through the wire, killing a man instantly while he talked on his telephone inside of his own house!

GHOST LIGHTS?

The famed St. Louis Lights are lights that seemingly appear out of nowhere near St. Louis, Saskatchewan. They have been theorized to be everything from light beams from distant car headlights reflected through the atmosphere to the lantern of a ghostly railroad-man killed in an accident.

HAUNTED BY THE GHOSTS OF THOUSANDS!

The autopsy table from the tuberculosis sanatorium near Fort Qu'Appelle is said to be haunted! When not being used for one of the thousands of autopsies, it witnessed over the years, it was said to be heard sliding across the floor of the room in which it was kept.

STRANGE BEDFELLOWS!

SASKATOON HAS STREETS NAMED AFTER SUCH VASTLY DIFFERENT CELEBRITIES AS PRIME MINISTER JOHN DIEFENBAKER, PLAYMATE OF THE YEAR SHANNON TWEED, PROFESSIONAL WRESTLER STU HART, AND THE PRINCE OF WALES!

The Paranormal Symposium is an annual event in Southern Saskatchewan that features lectures on the paranormal and séances, and visitors can buy everything from healing crystals to psychic readings!

A 6' 9" ROSE BY ANY OTHER NAME!

What do pro wrestlers Nitron, Big Sky, and Gully Gaspar have in common with horror movie star Tyler Mane? They are all the same person! They are all names used by Daryl Karolat of Saskatoon who stands nearly seven feet tall.

WHEN I SAID I NEEDED THREE PEICES OF I.D. I MEANT THEY NEEDED THE SAME NAME ON THEM!

WHO YA GONNA CALL?

Calling Lakes Paranormal Investigators (CLPI) is a business based in Fort Qu'Appelle that specializes in investigating paranormal activities such as haunted houses!

Under section 27 of the Saskatchewan Interpretation Act, which is used to interpret other laws in Saskatchewan, the definition of the word "cattle" includes horses!

MOST PEOPLE GO FROM SASKATOON TO CALGARY TO FIND SUCCESS, NOT THE OTHER WAY AROUND!

Professional wrestler and promoter Stu Hart was born in Saskatoon, but found his greatest fame in Calgary, Alberta as the promoter of Stampede Wrestling. His son, Bret Hart,was also a professional wrestler, but Bret was born in Calgary and found his greatest success in Saskatoon when he won his first world title there!

WE'VE HEARD OF SWITCH HITTING, BUT SWITCHING POSITIONS?

Terry Puhl of Melville, SK was one of the best outfielders in major league history and is a member of the Canadian Baseball Hall of Fame as an outfielder.

He was the most successful ball player to ever come out of Saskatchewan, but he was originally a pitcher! He was encouraged to switch to the outfield only after being signed by the Houston Astros, and never pitched in the majors despite being a championship winning amateur pitcher!

The largest fish ever caught in Saskatchewan was a Lake Sturgeon weighing 260 pounds (almost 120 kilograms).

Lana Nguyen gained a job as an engineering professor at the University of Regina by claiming to have earned a PhD that her ex-husband received. When confronted with the fact that her degree had been earned by a man, she claimed that she had had a sex change operation before she finally admitted to the truth and was charged with fraud.

After World War I ended, there were many army veterans on the Regina Rugby Club who had been wounded in the war. During one game in Calgary in 1919, a Regina player lost his glass eye and the game was stopped until it could be found. The player replaced it in his eye socket, and continued playing.

THE MOST BORING PLAYOFF GAMES IN HISTORY!

The Regina Rugby Club was set to play the 1911 Western Semi-final in Winnipeg, but they postponed the trip when the Winnipeg club advised them of bad weather. The Winnipeg team then claimed the win by default.

However, the Regina team went on to win the 1915 Western Final when the Saskatoon club was disqualified for not paying its league dues of $25!

BUT IF ONLY ONE TEAM SHOWS UP, CAN WE AT LEAST GET HALF OF THE TICKET PRICE BACK?

Rabid football fans are not a new phenomena in Saskatchewan. A 1911 rugby game between the Saskatoon and Regina clubs included a riot when the hometown Saskatoon fans attacked the Regina team.

The Saskatoon City police did not protect the visiting team, as policemen were among those taking part.

THE MOST BORING PLAYOFF GAMES IN HISTORY!

The 1919 Western Final was one of the slowest in history. When the Regina Rugby Club travelled to Calgary in November, a chinook had melted the frozen field and the teams had to play in two inches of mud!

In 1921, the head coach and general manager
of the Regina Rugby club were: Jerry Crapper and
Heinie Rogers!

In 1887, James Gaddy and Moise Racette, a pair of horse
thieves, shot and killed a homesteader near Qu'Appelle
when he tried to recover his stolen horse. They were
captured because they had previously had their photo taken
together and failed to pay the photographer for their prints.
The photographer simply gave the photos to the police when
he learned of their crime, and the police easily found them.

33

THE MILD WE$T!

In 1886, George Garnet became Saskatchewan's only stage coach robber. After stopping the stagecoach and robbing its passengers at gunpoint, he apparently felt guilty and gave them their money back, and then shared a bottle of whiskey with them.

He was later arrested for this crime and others, and bragged to a cell mate where he hid the loot. The cell mate was later released and stole the loot, and was in turn robbed and murdered by an unknown party.

The money was never recovered and Garnett received 14 years in prison.

34

In 1883, an editorial in the Regina daily newspaper wondered why so few arrests were being made in the city for prostitution when police officers could be seen coming and going from known brothels on a regular basis.

On the morning of May 14, 1891, Edward Fletcher was a witness in the trial of Jeff Prongua who was charged with killing cattle and selling illegal liquor, presided by Judge McGuire Battleford. Later that same afternoon, the same Edward Fletcher went on trial in the same courthouse before the same judge for murder!

In 1898, two RCMP officers recognized a black one-legged man on a train passing through town as being a wanted murderer from Ontario, and proudly arrested him. They quickly released him when they were told by the police officer travelling with the murderer that he had already arrested the murderer in British Columbia and was taking him back to Ontario.

In 1873, American wolf trappers killed between 15 and 20 Natives in what became known as the Cypress Hills Massacre. The incident led to the formation of the North West Mounted Police, later known as the Royal Canadian Mounted Police, in part because by the time the news of the crime reached Ottawa, the number of dead had been exaggerated to 200! Although men were charged with the murders, nobody was ever convicted.

MINUTES TO DESTROY, DECADES TO REPAY!

On June 30, 1912, a cyclone destroyed almost 500 buildings in Regina in a matter of minutes. The cost of rebuilding the city was so great that it was not fully paid for by the city until 1959!

Although he claimed not to have done the crime, he claimed he could use a deck of cards to mystically find out who committed the crime if he was given whiskey. After being given liquor, he led the police to the murder weapon and money stolen from the victim. After being arrested, he confessed to the crime.

41

URBAN SUBURBAN.

In 1785, the Hudson Bay Company built a trading post called South Branch House near what is now St. Louis. The rival French North West Company immediately built a competing trading post directly across the river from it.

In 1913, construction of the La Colle dam near Prince Albert was delayed because of high costs and stopped in 1914 because of World War I. Most of the lumber and cement that was stored at the site disappeared. By coincidence, many cellars were built in Prince Albert that year.

MOUNTAIN-EERING!

In order to host the 1971 Canada Winter Games, Saskatchewan had to build a mountain! 800,000 cubic yards of dirt was moved in order to build Mount Blackstrap for skiing events. In order to make the fake mountain look more real, 1,500 trees were planted around it.

There is a long history of alcohol and other goods being smuggled into Canada from the United States, but during the Great Depression of the 1930s, Saskatchewan farmers smuggled grain into the States, to take advantage of the higher prices being paid there.

FOOLS GOLD!

In 1914, two gold prospectors arrived in Battleford with an extremely rich ore sample. They refused to tell anyone where they found it, and the secret died with them when they were both killed in a storm shortly thereafter. It is unknown if the gold was ever found by anyone else.

Count Berthold Von Imhoff was a famous artist throughout Europe in the late 1800s and early 1900s, and painted portraits of royalty. However, the largest gallery of his work is located at his old farm near St. Walburg, Saskatchewan, where he lived the last third of his life.

In August of 1944, a cyclone struck Kamsack with such force that a freight car was hurled through the local train station!

When the North West Mounted Police was first formed, one of its duties was mail delivery to settlers.

The first Mountie to die in the line of duty was killed in Saskatchewan. In 1879, Constable Marmaduke Graburn was shot in the back near Cypress Hills. Although a local man was charged with the crime, he was not only found not guilty at trial but was later hired by the North West Mounted Police as a scout.

In 1914, a notice appeared in the Estevan Progress suggesting to swimmers in the nearby river that their "anatomy be clothed, draped, or painted in such a manner as not to mar the landscape."

In 1915, Jacob Lemm of Estevan was convicted of smuggling other German immigrants into the United States from Canada so they could return to Germany and fight against Canada and its allies in World War I!

Before the formation of the North West Mounted Police in 1873, the enforcement of law in the area that became Saskatchewan was the responsibility of the Hudson Bay Company. It built its own jails and had employees with the power to act as judges in criminal cases and on two occasions ordered that convicted murderers be hanged.

The Western Development Museum not only has over
78,000 artifacts either on display in its four locations
covering a total of 24,422 square meters or in storage,
it has an undetermined number of ghosts attached to these
artifacts!Ghostly experiences in the Saskatoon, Moose Jaw,
and North Battleford locations have included flying objects,
apparitions, light anomalies, ghosts appearing in photo-
graphs, and disembodied voices! For unknown reasons,
none of this has occurred in the Yorkton location.

Saskatchewan Ghost-Hunters Society Inc. is an organization formed in 2008 "to dismiss or validate the presence or existence of spirit haunting through investigation."

DOOR SERVICE?!

In 1958, an employee of a Weyburn newspaper went door to door to local businesses, trying to sell them advertising space in the paper. He was later convicted of 16 charges of theft for stealing from the businesses he visited and selling the items at a second hand store.

On April 1, 1981, a Weyburn newspaper received complaints about photos allegedly showing freight cars hauling water from Lake Erie to Weyburn when the town was struck by drought, even though the photographer was credited as being an April fool joke!

One traditional Plains Indian religious belief was that evil
shamans were capable of magically shooting an object
such as a pebble into someone they disliked, causing disease.
The curing ritual involved a good shaman magically sucking
the object out of the diseased person using a hollow tube.

The first movie shown in Saskatchewan was exhibited in a second floor auditorium of the City Hall on August 16 and 17, 1897.

The first movie banned in Saskatchewan was the 1910 film of the world championship boxing match between Jack Johnson and Jim Jeffries. Such movies were denounced in a letter to the premier of Saskatchewan by a prominent reverend stating that such movies were "universally acknowledged to be very demoralizing to the people, particularly the young." Luckily, this reverend did not live to see the day when people could watch MMA on television 24 hours a day.

A 1912 Saskatchewan law prohibited any movie being shown on a Sunday except in connection with a religious service and with a special permit. It also banned showing any movie at any time that showed crime or prize fighting.

In the 1870s, mail from Fort Walsh to Battleford had to go through either Edmonton or Winnipeg, so the mail travelled three to four times the distance between the two settlements.

BLEAK AND TREELESS PLAIN

The location of Regina was chosen by the Canadian Pacific Railway. The location was described by the Saskatchewan Herald in 1882 as "standing… in a bleak and treeless plain" and "however rich the soil, the lack of wood and water in the vicinity must militate against it becoming a place of very great importance."

In 1890, a local company began supplying electricity to the city of Regina for the first time. However, the street lights were only turned on for Saturday nights.

Archie Belaney, the Englishman who became known as the Saskatchewan writer Grey Owl, once decided to get himself fired from an office job by setting off a small explosion in the fireplace of the company where he worked.

In 1879, the RCMP hired local natives to build a fort for protection. In 1885, some of those same natives took part in an attack against the same fort.

Mrs. Hoburg, a restaurant owner in Moose Jaw in the 1880s, smuggled alcohol into the town from Winnipeg by travelling by train with a rubber tube around her stomach filled with illegal booze. She also decorated a whiskey keg to look like a pillow!

DR. JAMES HECTOR,

The Palliser expedition of 1857-60, which explored Western Canada, including parts of what later became Saskatchewan, included Dr. James Hector, who served as both geologist and surgeon on the trip.

During the 1870s, alcohol was prohibited in Fort Walsh and any alcohol that was found was seized by the North West Mounted Police and poured on the ground.

According to legend, it was often poured out over a metal tub that was hidden under dead branches, so the Mounties could later retrieve it!

During the Riel Rebellion, the Canadian government hired an American soldier, Lieutenant Howard, to fight in the Battle of Batoche. He was paid $400 to operate a Gatling gun, a machine gun that could fire 120 rounds a minute.

The first time the red cross symbol was used by Canadian troops was in the Riel Rebellion. Two strips of red cloth were sewn onto a covered wagon that was being used as an ambulance to take the wounded to safety.

According to legend, the wheat crop of 1915 was so dense that farmers could walk on top of their crop without bending the stalks!

Snow drifts were so high in the winter of 1906-07 that cattle could wander into trees and become trapped in the branches. When spring finally came, dead cattle were hanging 20 to 30 feet off the ground!

In 1907, a Cypress Hills rancher thought a cow had wandered off during the winter and died. It had actually wandered into the United States and joined a larger herd, and when that herd was shipped to Chicago for sale, the Canadian brand was identified and the true owner received a cheque for his missing cow!

A 1921 Rugby game between the Saskatoon and Regina clubs had to be replayed because the referees had made a bad call. Because there was no instant replay in those days, fans had to sign affidavits swearing to what had happened!

SAFETY EQUIPMENT?

In a 1923 rugby game, a Regina player was almost killed by his helmet! His leather helmet was secured by a thin lace around his chin, and when the helmet was knocked back on his head during a play, the lace almost strangled him until it was cut off his throat!

He refused to wear a helmet for the rest of his career.

The Regina Rugby club made it to the 1923 Grey Cup, but almost had to leave its star player behind! He was a CNR employee, and he refused to travel on the CPR train that had been booked to take the team to the game in Ontario!

In 1924, the Regina Rugby Club changed its name to the Regina Roughriders, and later to the Saskatchewan Roughriders.

The club had almost changed its name in 1915, but couldn't because a local lacrosse team was already called the Roughriders!

A 1929 Roughrider playoff game had to be delayed because the referee tripped in a gopher hole and knocked himself unconscious!

HE ALSO KNOCKED ME OUT! I SUED THE TEAM AND SETTLED OUT OF COURT WHEN THEY PROMISED TO MAKE MY GRANDSON GAINER THE TEAM MASCOT!

Gary Tinker of Pinehouse, Saskatchewan was born with cerebral palsy. In 1989, to raise awareness of the needs of disabled people living in Northern Saskatchewan, he walked 650 kilometres on his crutches from his home to Regina. In 2009, he celebrated the 20th anniversary of his walk by going skydiving!

Alvin Law, originally of Yorkton, Saskatchewan who was born without arms, learned to play the trombone, drums, and piano with his feet, and became a successful inspirational speaker, has also had such roles as radio personality, professional actor, and civil servant.

He also helped raise $150,000,000 for charity!

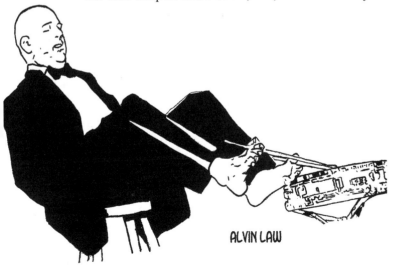

ALVIN LAW

Dene is a language spoken by some Native people in Northern Saskatchewan. The language has no similarities to the Cree language spoken by aboriginals elsewhere in Saskatchewan, but is very similar to the Apache language spoken in Arizona and the Lipan language found in Texas!

Brian Painchaud was 10 when he starred in Who Has Seen the Wind?, which was the highest grossing Canadian movie of 1977, and which was filmed in Saskatchewan. He never made another film and died only 10 years later.

Reindeer Lake, located in Northern Saskatchewan, is 239 kilometres long at its longest point. By comparison, Regina and Saskatoon are 259 kilometres apart!

Popular cartoon character Homer Simpson is loosely based on Matt Groening's real life father, Homer Groening of Main Centre, Saskatchewan. According to the 2006 census, Main Centre is no longer a main centre, as it has an official population of zero!

The popular cartoon show Atomic Betty was set in the fictional suburb of Moose Jaw Heights.

DEATH IN THE SKIES!

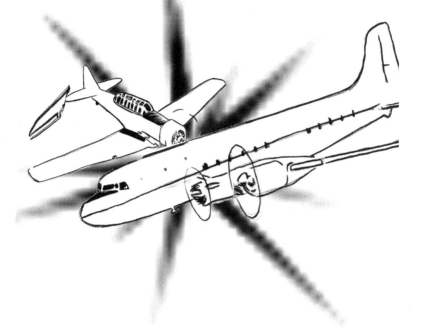

In 1954, a military plane collided with a commercial flight over Moose Jaw. Although all 36 people on board the two planes were killed, amazingly only one person on the ground was killed because much of the wreckage fell on a golf course, and the bulk of one airplane landed on only one house, missing a nearby school with 350 students.

In 1930, Robert "Stonewall" Jackson became the first black Roughrider. A star on the field, he completed one cold practice wearing a scarf over his helmet and mitts on his hands, and on one run, ducked through a hole in the fence at Taylor Field and headed for the warmth of the dressing room!

In 1931, the Roughriders forgot to ship their uniforms to the Western Semi-final in Winnipeg, so they were forced to play the game with equipment borrowed from the opposition!

The first dinosaur fossil found in Canada was hadrosaurs found in the Wood Mountain area in Saskatchewan in 1874.

HADROSAURS WERE DUCK-BILLED DINOSAURS.

The name Saskatchewan is derived from a First Nation's word meaning "swiftly moving river." Nobody is sure why a province consisting mainly of grasslands and trees would be named after a body of water.

The largest hailstone that ever fell in Canada was in Saskatchewan in 1973. It weighed 290 grams and was roughly the size of a grapefruit!

The official motto of Canada, "From Sea to Sea" was adopted by the federal government in 1921, but its first use by a Canadian government was by the Saskatchewan legislature in 1906.

The first government prepaid medical plan in Canada was in the Rural Municipality of McKillop, Saskatchewan in 1939. The plan did not become province-wide until 1946.

HOCKEY FIGHT IN CANADA!

The all-time NHL leader in penalty minutes is Dave "Tiger" Williams of Saskatchewan. The record holder for most penalty minutes in a season is Dave "The Hammer" Schultz, also of Saskatchewan. Although Schultz averaged 25 fights a year in the NHL, he had only two fights in his entire three year junior hockey career. !

DAVE TIGER WILLIAMS

DAVE "THE HAMMER" SCHULTZ

Not only did Saskatchewan once have a village named Titanic, it still has a town named after a Titanic passenger. Melville was named after Sir Charles Melville, a railroad president who died when the famous ship sank.

ROADSIDE FASHION

According to a 2009 news story, Gary Armsworthy of Regina made fur hats, mitts, and slippers from fur he scavenged from road kill.

Although wolves are considered to be dangerous animals, between 1950 and 2005 there was only one recorded instance of a wolf killing a human. That was near Points North Landing, Saskatchewan. By comparison, between 1999 and 2002, there were six people in Saskatchewan killed in car accidents involving animals. Most of these accidents involved moose and deer, which are considered to be harmless animals!

During the 1945 season, there were so few Roughrider uniforms that players leaving the field had to give their jerseys to the players coming onto the field.

99

Arnold Boldt of Saskatoon lost a leg in a farming accident at age three and went on to set multiple world records in the one-legged high jump and long jump, as well as multiple paracycling championships. As a university student, he competed in track meets against athletes with two legs, and at age 52 continues to compete in cycling, often against opponents with two legs.

ARNOLD BOLT

BOLDT'S HIGHEST JUMP IN COMPETITION WAS 2.08 METRES.

THE NOT SO GREAT ESCAPE!

During World War I, the federal government had 24 prisoner of war camps in Canada, one of which was in Saskatchewan. The Eaton Internment Camp was a complete disaster. Hastily constructed, it was also hastily taken apart after only 24 days because the prisoners refused to work, the guards were undisciplined, and there was a successful escape during that short time. The prisoners were transported to another camp in Nova Scotia.

TRUE LEADERSHIP!

In 1947, American Fred Grant joined the Roughriders as a running back. However, because of the league's import rules, he was ineligible to play. Rather than sending Grant back to the United States, head coach Ken Preston became a player again and made Grant the head coach!

In 1947, the name of the Riders' home field was changed to Taylor Field. The field had natural grass. The groundskeeper was provided with a rake, hoe, and wheelbarrow by the club, but was forced to borrow a lawn mower.

In 1948, the Roughriders changed their team colours from red and black to green and white. The reason for the change? They needed new uniforms, and a board member found a large number of green and white jerseys on sale at a war surplus sale in Chicago!

Gainer the Gopher was not the first Roughrider mascot. In 1949, the mascot was Ruffie the Goat. Instead of a man in a costume, it was a real goat wearing a green and white blanket.

An ancient Cree story greatly resembles the story of Noah from the Bible, although it may predate it. After the Creator has caused a great flood that covered the world, Wisakedjak and three animals that survived the flood (an otter, a beaver, and a muskrat), rebuilt the world!

Candle Lake is named for a Cree legend of flickering lights appearing near the north end of the lake. Explanations for this range from a bad omen caused by the dead to gas emitted by decaying driftwood.

For most hockey players a hat trick means
scoring three goals in one game. The Gordie
Howe Hat Trick means a player has one goal,
one assist, and one fight in the same game.
Howe was born in Floral, SK and still holds
the record for most NHL games played.

The village of Shiloh Saskatchewan was founded in 1910 by a dozen African American families who moved from Oklahoma to escape racial segregation. At its peak, the village consisted of 50 African American families, all of whom later left the area for larger centres.

The Shiloh cemetery is the only African American cemetery in Saskatchewan.

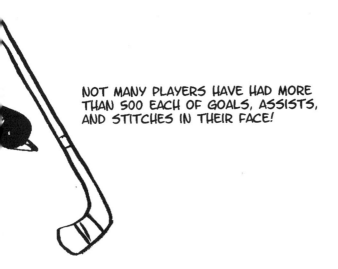

NOT MANY PLAYERS HAVE HAD MORE THAN 500 EACH OF GOALS, ASSISTS, AND STITCHES IN THEIR FACE!

On August 15, 1887, a two and a half year old child wandered away from its Regina home and was found two days later hiding in some bushes, apparently having wandered 1.5 miles on its own without being seen or helped by anyone. The child did not suffer from any ill effects from the outing.

According to North West Mounted Police reports from Regina in 1884, a man convicted of manslaughter could receive a sentence of as little as six months in jail, while criminals convicted of bringing stolen horses into Canada from the United States could expect to receive penitentiary sentences of two to five years!

According to an 1889 report from the North West Mounted Police, (NWMP) there were only two major crimes that year in the Battleford area. One of them, involving the theft of 39 gallons of beer, was committed by two constables of the NWMP!

Newspapers in the early 20th century often printed material that would be considered politically incorrect today. In 1912, the Saskatchewan Star's headline about the sinking of the Titanic read "Men of Anglo-Saxon race face death in heroic manner" while a 1921 letter to the editor of that newspaper said in part "There are certain Jews in this province engaged in the liquor trade who could contribute a great deal to Saskatchewan by leaving it at once."

Until 1921, most Saskatchewan small towns had no police presence. When a crime did occur, which was rare, a telegram was sent to the nearest RCMP detachment, and a Mountie would travel to the town on the next train!

The Bronfman family, heir to the Seagram's liquor company fortune, began its journey to becoming one of the wealthiest families in Canada in Saskatchewan.

The first Bronfmans to immigrate to Canada from Russia homesteaded near Wapella, Saskatchewan!

In 1923, the Regina Leader-Post claimed that there were more illegal stills in Saskatchewan than in all the rest of the country combined!

THE ORIGINAL BIG SCREEN!

In the 1920s and 1930s, daily newspapers in Regina and Saskatoon had playboards erected on their buildings so they could act out the World Series games for onlookers. Crowds of up to 2,000 people would gather to watch a six foot by six foot piece of wood as men behind it manipulated ball and player symbols with magnets as the play by play action was announced over a loudspeaker!

YOU'VE HEARD OF SWITCH HITTERS, BUT A SWITCH PITCHER?

Bill Frost, of Melfort, competed in baseball tournaments in Saskatchewan in the 1930s and could pitch equally well with his right or left hand!

THE MOST VERSATILE FEMALE ATHLETE OF ALL TIME HAD A SASKATCHEWAN CONNECTION!

BABE DIDRIKSON

Babe Didrikson, who won Olympic medals in track and field, held the world record for throwing a softball, and played professional golf, once ran a race against Dean Griffing of the Saskatchewan Roughriders and won!

IN MY DEFENCE, I WAS AN OFFENSIVE LINEMAN, NOT A RUNNING BACK! WHY WOULDN'T THEY LET ME TAKE HER ON IN WEIGHTLIFTING?

The movie Field of Dreams, which was about the members
the Chicago White Sox who tried to fix the 1919 World Se
could have been set in Saskatchewan. Eight members of
the team, who were nicknamed the Black Sox, were banne
from baseball, two of them had a Saskatchewan connection

Swede Risberg and Happy Felsch played for a team based
North Dakota that toured Saskatchewan, where their lifetin
ban was not in force. (Felsch played the 1927 season with a
Regina team)

The movie A League of Their Own, which starred Geena Davis, Madonna, and Rosie O'Donnell, had a Saskatchewan connection. The movie was about the All-American Girls Professional Baseball League, which was far from all American. Of the 545 girls who played in the league, 25 were from Saskatchewan.

Wicca, a religious practice that is a non-Satanic version of witchcraft, has groups in Saskatchewan that follow its beliefs. "Jane," a green witch interviewed for this book – who specializes in healing the mind, soul, and body with plants and crystals – did not want her real name revealed because of continuing prejudice against Wiccans.

WELL, I DON'T BELIEVE IN THE HEALING POWERS OF CRYSTALS, SO THERE! NEH!

WICCANS DO NOT ACKNOWLEDGE THE CHRISTIAN IDEA OF SATAN AT ALL.

AH-OO, WEREWOLVES OF... REGINA?

There are people who believe themselves to be werewolves, at least in a spiritual sense. They feel a strong connection with wolves and see aspects of that animal in their personalities and actions.

MANY PLANTS FOUND IN SASKATCHEWAN HAVE SYMBOLISM IN THE WICCAN RELIGION, INCLUDING:

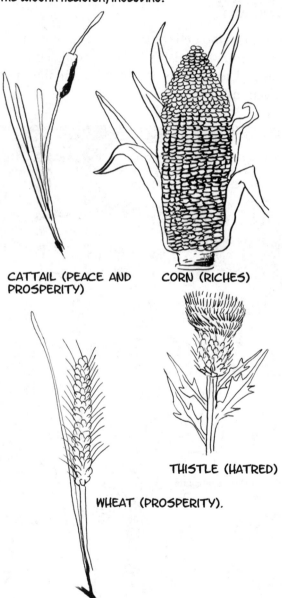

CATTAIL (PEACE AND PROSPERITY)

CORN (RICHES)

THISTLE (HATRED)

WHEAT (PROSPERITY).

DAISY (INNOCENCE),

NETTLE (CRUELTY)

FLAX (FEELING SOMEONE ELSE'S KINDNESS)

WELL, WHEAT MAKES ME PROSPEROUS, I HATE THISTLE, AND I'M CRUEL TO NETTLES, SO MAYBE THERE IS SOMETHING TO THIS WICCA STUFF. SIGN ME UP!

VAMPIRES ON THE PRAIRIES!

Psyvamps are people who believe that they can feed off the psychic energy of others to harmlessly bring themselves peace of mind and healing.

Several Regina people who were interviewed for this book report real life encounters with ghosts. A Regina woman, who wishes to remain anonymous, witnessed her brother's death, and since then has seen his spirit when stressed and in her dreams. Another Regina resident was warned by his late mother in a dream to avoid a certain place, and an assault occurred on someone else at that place within a week.

HAUNTED HOUSES AREN'T JUST FOUND ON THE MIDWAY!

Regina residents have reported such incidents of their homes being haunted as ghosts peacefully singing to children, practical joker ghosts who will open oven doors when people are trying to leave the house, and the ghost of a pet who will wake its old owner so it can have its old spot in the bed to itself.

TIMES WOULD CHANGE, AND FAST!

Public opinion on working married women in Saskatchewan has changed with time. A letter to Saskatoon city council dated October 16, 1931 read in part: "The great majority of employed married women are working just so they can get away from their husbands and have a good time." A letter to the editor of the Saskatoon StarPhoenix dated June 28, 1930 stated: "Supposing we all practiced the selfish economy of married couples working; what would be the result? The world will sink into oblivion."

THEN WORLD WAR II STARTED LATER IN THE 1930S, MARRIED WOMEN WERE ENCOURAGED TO WORK, AND THE WRITERS OF THESE LETTERS WERE NEVER HEARD FROM AGAIN!

On September 27, 1922, two series of explosions rocked Moosomin, Saskatchewan as bank robbers blew up a bank vault and the safe within the vault. Citizens of the small town were so frightened that nobody thought to call the police and the robbers easily escaped.

A JOE BY ANY OTHER NAME!

Griffiths Stadium at the University of Saskatchewan was named after Joe Griffiths, the long-time Physical Director of the University. Although he was widely known as Joe, his name was actually Ernest Wynne Griffiths.

FROM SASKATOON TO MOSCOW!

Although born in Ontario, Charles Hay, the man who as President of Hockey Canada helped make the 1972 Canada-USSR hockey series happen, had a Saskatchewan connection. He saw his first hockey game when his family moved to Saskatoon in 1913, and in his own words "I got hooked."

TRAVELLING LIGHT!

Doctor Thomas Neatby has been described as immigrating from London, England to Earl Gray, Saskatchewan in 1906, with little more than his wife, nurse, eight children, a satchel of medical equipment, and a personal library of over 3,000 books!

JUST ONE OF THE BOYS!

In the early 1900s in Saskatchewan, the word "boy" was used to include any grown man who was unmarried!

In the early 1900s, most teachers in Saskatchewan only had a second class teaching certificate, which meant they had an education consisting of Grade 11 and one term of training at "normal school."

AT LEAST IT WAS EASY TO TAKE ATTENDANCE!

When the school of physical education opened at the University of Saskatchewan in 1933, its faculty outnumbered its students five to three! Originally, the school only accepted female students.

THE ORIGINAL ICE DANCERS!

During the 1920s in Swift Current, figure skating was considered a "sissy" activity, so instead young people would gather at the skating rink on Saturdays for Music Night, where they would waltz and fox trot on hockey skates!

THEY CALLED HIM THE ONE MAN TRACK TEAM!

In 1946, Bob Evans of the University of Saskatchewan, competed in most of the events of the first interuniversity track and field competition between Saskatchewan, Alberta, and Manitoba, and accumulated as many points as the entire Alberta team! This actually caused a rule change, which limited the number of events one athlete could compete in during future competitions!

SO I COULD KEEP COMPETING IN AS MANY EVENTS AS POSSIBLE, I JUST SWITCHED TO THE DECATHLON AND MADE THE 1952 CANADIAN OLYMPIC TEAM!

ATHLETIC AND FUNNY!

Diane Jones of Saskatoon was married to John Konihowski of the Edmonton Eskimos and was a world class competitor in the pentathlon. After winning a gold medal at the 1978 Commonwealth Games, she stated "Next to marrying a Ukranian Eskimo, this is the greatest thing that's ever happened to me.

I WAS ALSO FAVORED TO WIN A GOLD MEDAL IN THE 1980 OLYMPICS UNTIL CANADA WITHDREW ITS ENTIRE TEAM FROM THE GAMES AS PART OF AN INTERNATIONAL BOYCOTT!

POETRY IN MOTION!

An early Saskatchewan homesteader wrote of his new
home:
Saskatchewan, you always seem to me
A woman without favour in your face
Flat breasted, angular, devoid of grace.
Why do men woo you? Naught is fair to see
In that wide visage with unkempt hair,
And form that squarely stands, feet splayed apart.

WARNING SIGN!

Signs in each room of a Maple Creek motel used to read:
When the wind blows, please hang on to the door.

THE EXPLORER WITH THE HEART OF A POET!

The first European to reach the Saskatchewan River was Henry Kelsey in 1691. Unfortunately, his journals were misplaced by the Hudson's Bay Company for more than 200 years and were not published until 1929!

During the early 1900s in Saskatchewan, homesteaders would make their own curling stones out of pickle pails or chamber pots filled with cement!

A HIGH POINT OF VISITING SASKATCHEWAN!!

The Cypress Hills are the highest point in Canada between Labrador and the Rockies. They contain 50 species of plants and animals not found anywhere else in Canada!

A STICKY PROBLEM!

Regina is built on gumbo clay, which becomes incredibly sticky when wet. Before Regina's streets were paved, it was estimated that more rubber boots had been lost there than in any other city in Canada!

MAYBE IT WAS BECAUSE WE HAD TO HOP SO MUCH THAT HOPSCOTCH BECAME SO POPULAR IN REGINA!

A BAD HABIT!

When the Ku Klux Klan was trying to discredit the Catholic Church in Saskatchewan, legend has it that it paid prostitutes in Moose Jaw to dress up as nuns!

In 1915, Scottish artist James Henderson moved to the outskirts of Fort Qu'Appelle and spent the next 50 years painting nothing but scenes of the Qu'Appelle Valley!

HE HAD GREAT HORSE SENSE!

Saskatchewan poet Stanley Harrison's book Gentlemen, the Horse! consisted of nothing but poems about horses!

During the time Sitting Bull's band of Sioux from the United States spent time in Saskatchewan, among the goods they used to trade for supplies were watches taken from dead cavalry men after the battle of Little Big Horn. During his time in Canada, Sitting Bull was praised by those who met him as peaceful, reserved, and dignified, and caused no trouble this side of the border.

EVERYONE LOVES A PARADE!

The first nude parade in Saskatchewan occurred in Yorkton in 1903. The parade was a protest by Doukhobors against government opposition to their beliefs.

In the 1890's, there was a colony of Scottish Herbrideans near Saltcoats. The colony only lasted approximately 30 years as the immigrants were traditionally fishermen, not farmers, and they spoke only gaelic, not english.

Maybe weathermen of today should try to make their forecasts come true! During 1937, the worst year of the 1930's drought, when temperatures reached 114 degrees and topsoil was blown off fields and into ditches, Chief Sheepskin of the Wood Mountian Reserve performed a traditional rain dance.

It rained for the first time that year, unfortunately, the elderly chief died shortly after his dance.

Saskatoon became a city in 1906. By 1907, the city's credit was so bad that the only way the water system could be completed was for the mayor to personally secure a loan for $30, 000.